Ski Trip

Children's travel activity and keepsake book

***Topher** is named after St. Chris**topher**, the patron saint for travellers who is known for keeping all those who travel safe from harm.

tinytourists is all about inspiring family travel and making the most of adventures; keeping travel meaningful and memorable, educational and fun. Visit us on Facebook to find out more and to join the tinytourists' community.

Written and Designed by Louise Amodio
Illustrated by Louise Amodio and Catherine Mantle
Cover Illustration by Isabella (age 5).

Published by Beans and Joy Publishing Ltd as a product from Tiny Tourists Ltd, Great Britain.
www.beansandjoy.com

ISBN: 978 0-9954949-6-1

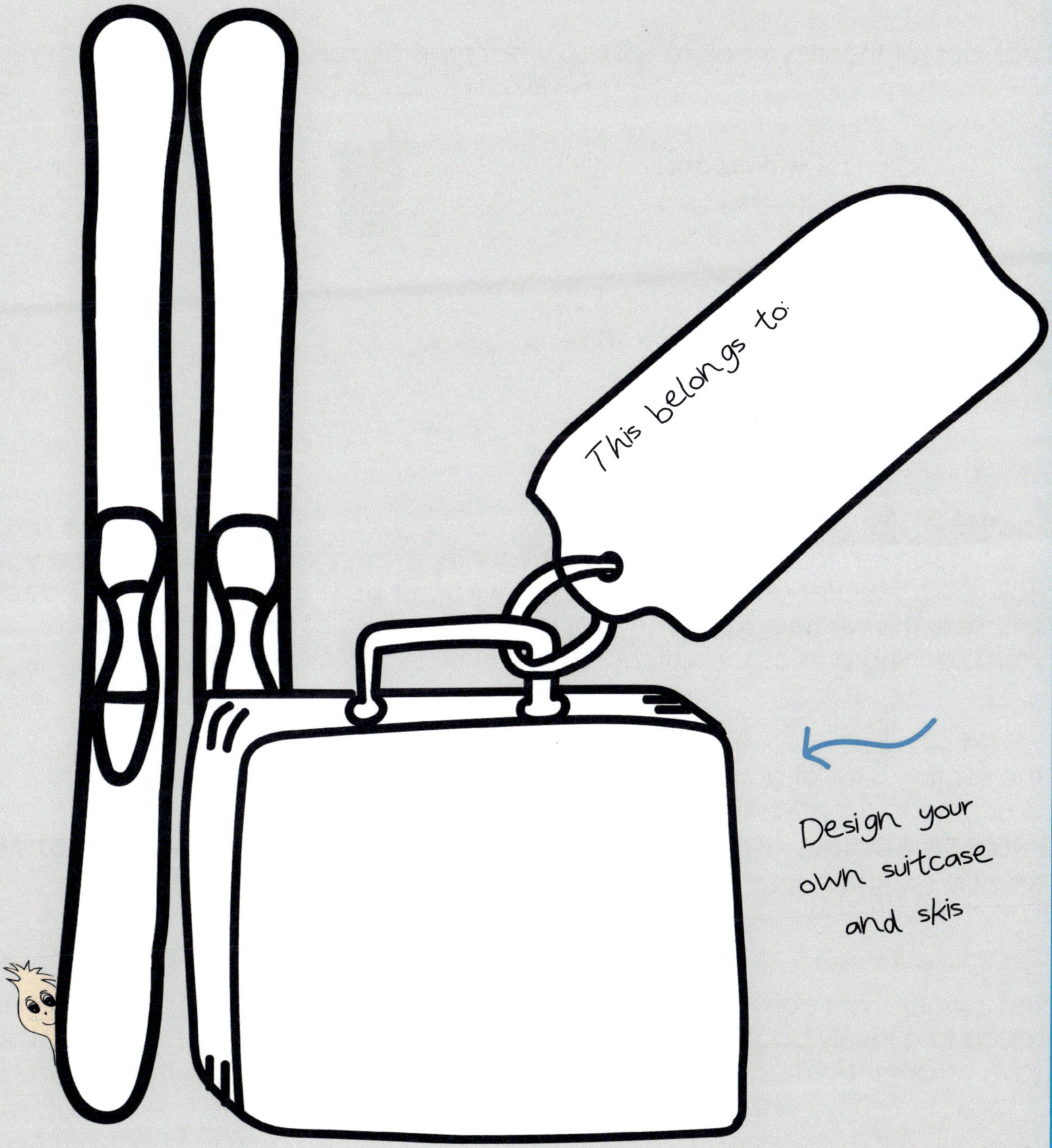

This belongs to:

Design your
own suitcase
and skis

Your adventure starts here

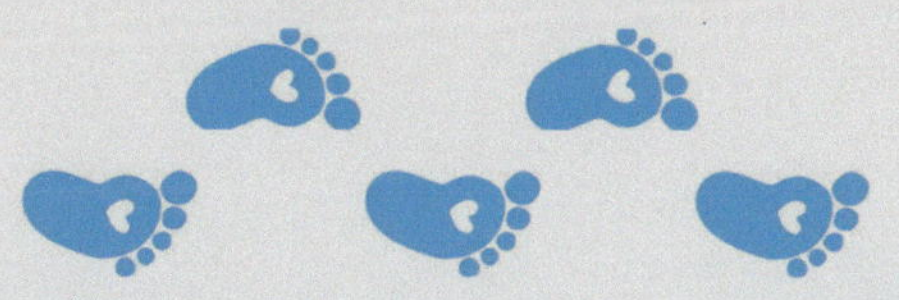

How to use this book

Welcome to your fun-packed travel activity book!

Look out for these symbols to tell you what type of activity you'll be doing:

 for writing and recording

 for drawing and colouring and being creative

Time to get started!

Section 1: My Travel Log
Use this section to start thinking about your trip; when you're going, where you're going, who you're going with, what the weather be like, and what you'll pack in your suitcase. This will help form part of a lovely keepsake as well as practice your planning and organisational skills!

Section 2: Epic Explorer Skills
This section is full of games and activities for a bit of ski-themed fun. All are designed to support skills you'll already have;

PROBLEM-SOLVING (MATHS), CODE-BREAKING (LITERACY AND LANGUAGES) AND SPY SKILLS (SCIENCE AND GEOGRAPHY). SEE INDEX FOR MORE DETAILS.

Section 3: Memory Bank
This is where you can record all the memories from your trip. The perfect finishing touch to a lovely book of holiday memories; what you did, what you ate, what you saw, what you collected, and fun lists for recording the best bits and the worst bits.

Happy Skiing!

My Info

Me:

My home address:

Eye Colour:

Hair Colour:

Distinguishing features:

How long is your right index finger?

0 1 2 3 4 5 6 7 8 9 10 11 12 13 14 15 16 cm

My Destination:

Arrival:

Date: ___________

Passport Stamp:

Departure:

Date: ___________

Where am I going?

Can you plot where you're going skiing on this world map?

Which big cities or countries will you go past or through or over on your journey there?

How will I get there?

For each method of transport you use to get to your destination, note how many hours you'll spend on each, and add it all up:

	Hours
Total:	

What am I taking with me?

Draw the 10 most important things you have packed in your suitcase?

Who am I going with?

Draw a picture of who you're going on holiday with in the frame below:

Example

Holiday Portrait

What will the weather be like?

Draw a circle around the weather you predict you'll have, and then record the actual weather you really do have:

What weather DID you have?
Was your prediction correct?

Epic Explorer Skills

PROBLEM-SOLVING (MATHS)

CODE-BREAKING (LITERACY & LANGUAGES)

SPY SKILLS (SCIENCE, GEOGRAPHY)

Your Flag

Can you complete this picture with the colours of the flag of the country you are visiting?

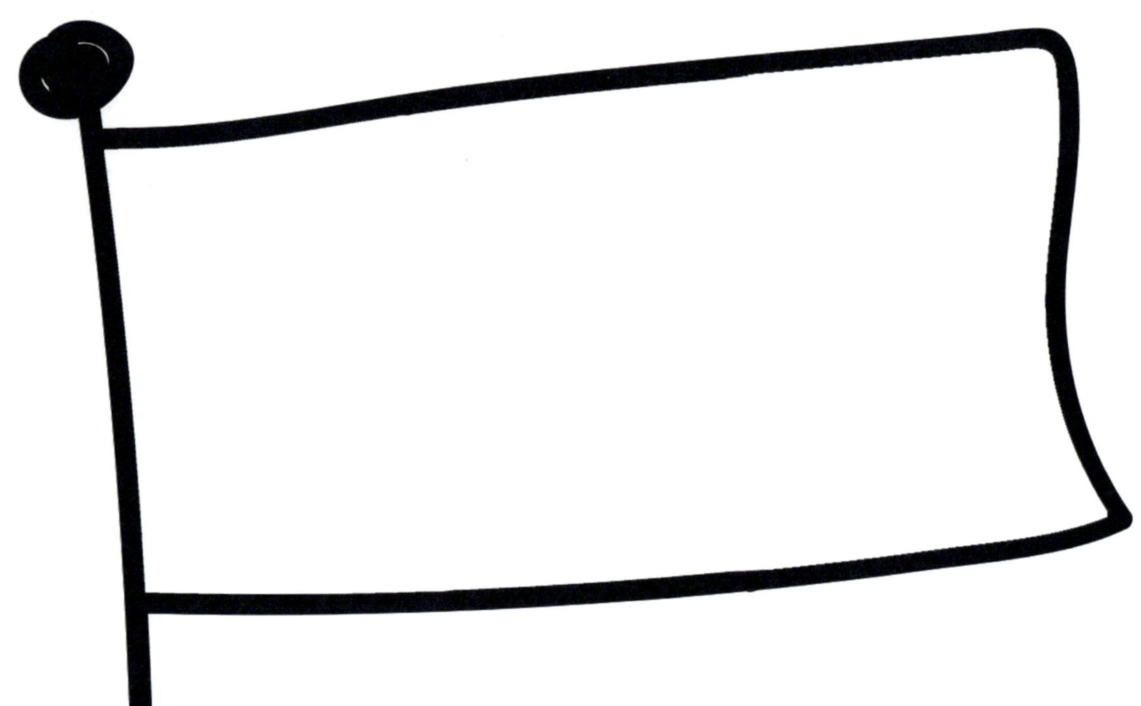

Hello! Please! Thank you!

What are the words for hello, please and thank you in the country you are visiting? Write them here and try to remember them:

Ski Resorts with "Altitude"

How high is the ski resort you're visiting? _____________ m

Match these high ski resorts with their country's flag:

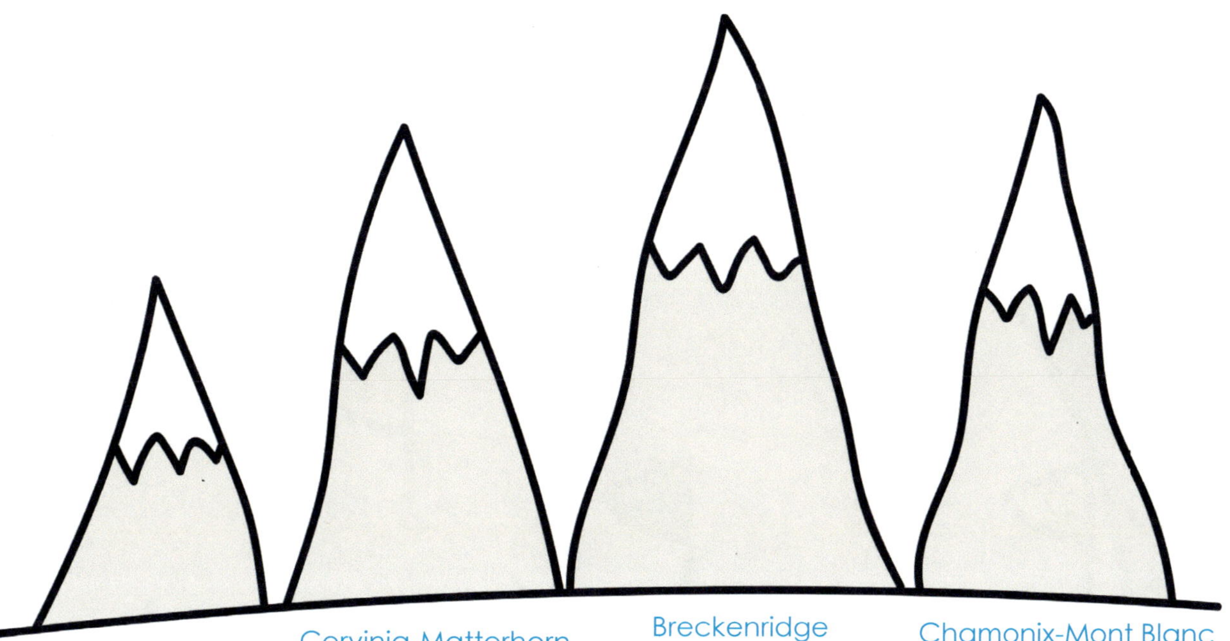

Ski Run 3

Starting at the top flag, number 3, draw a route down the mountain around all the flags that are in the 3 times table:

Ski Run 5

Starting at the top flag, number 5, draw a route down the mountain around all the flags that are in the 5 times table:

5
4
7
6
9
10
15
12
20
25
23
21
35
30
40
45
42
51

Snowball Prep !!

Some children are getting ready for a snowball fight.

Each child needs 10 snowballs.

Looking at what they have made already, write how many extra snowballs each needs to make until they have 10 and are ready to rumble!!

+ [ ] = 10

+ [ ] = 10

+ [ ] = 10

+ [ ] = 10

+ [ ] = 10

Snowball Fight !

Each of these children start with 10 snowballs and throw some snowballs at their friends.

Can you work out how many they will have left?

10 − =

10 − =

10 − =

10 − =

BIGGER Snowball Prep !!

Some children are getting ready for a snowball fight.

Each child needs 10 snowballs.

Looking at what they have made already, write how many extra snowballs each needs to make until they have 10 and are ready to rumble!!

$$\square + \square = 20$$

$$\square + \square = 20$$

$$\square + \square = 20$$

$$\square + \square = 20$$

$$\square + \square = 20$$

BIGGER Snowball Fight !

Each of these children start with 20 snowballs and throw some snowballs at their friends.

Can you work out how many they will have left?

20 − 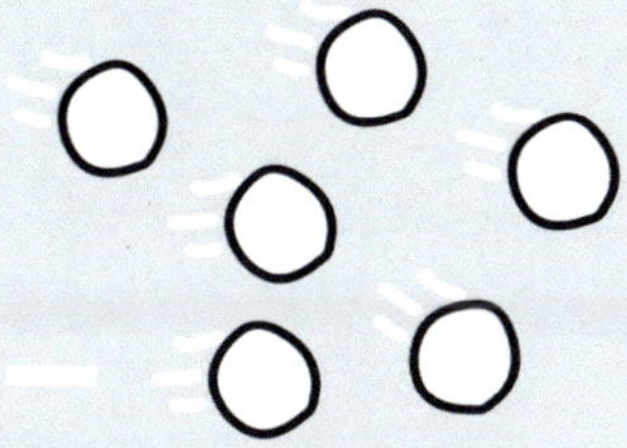 =

20 − 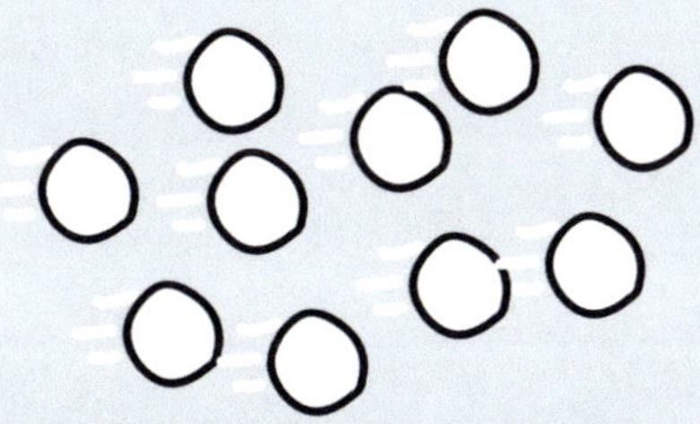 =

20 −  =

20 −  =

Build a Snowman?

It's time to build some snowmen.
Work out how many of each item you might need, then
add some faces and warm clothes to these three snowmen:

Scarves 3

Eyes

Buttons

Noses

Snow Snow Snow Snow !

There are lots of types of snow you might come across during your trip. See if you can find these words in the grid below:

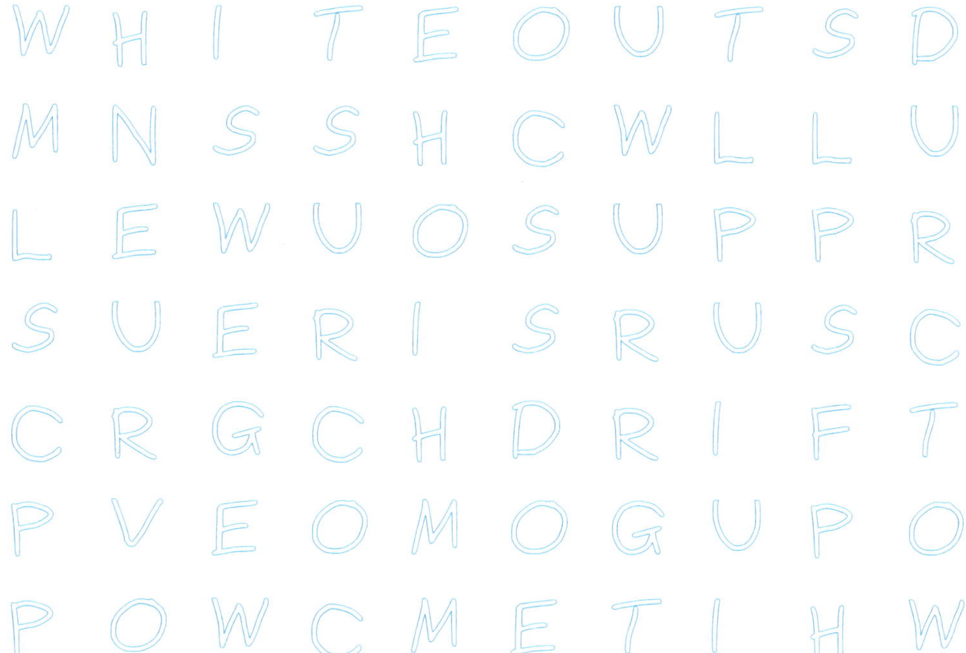

POWDER - soft snow, just fallen

MOGUL - bumps in the snow

DRIFT - where snow has blown into a pile

CRUST - a hard icy top surface to soft snow

CRUD - clumpy broken up snow

WHITEOUT - snowstorm with bad visibility

SLUSH - soft melting snow

ICE - frozen snow

EXPERIMENT

If you put a small cup of water outside in the cold at night, what happens to it by morning?

Snowman Silhouettes

Can you match each snowman with his shodow?

Snowman Shadow

A shadow is formed when something blocks the light coming from the sun or lightsource. Where it falls depends on where the sun is.

Can you draw a shadow for this snowman in the right place?

Hint: Look where the sun is

Ski Skills

When you learn to ski, you learn about how to go fast, how to slow down, how to turn, and how to stop safely.

How many differences can you see between these two skiers?

Who do you think is skiing the fastest?

Hint: Look at the position of their skis

Can you add some colour to their ski suits and skis ?

Who is my Instructor?

Three children need to find their ski instructor. They have been given a piece of paper describing what their instructor looks like.

Can you help to match them up to the right one?

Claude

Loves stripes

Got a new yellow helmet last week

Has brown hair

Giancarlo

Hates stripes

Borrowed his sister's pink gloves

Has the same skis as Hugo.

Hugo

Has green saloppettes

Has gloves to match his salopettes

Has a lovely green scarf too.

# Winter Season

The mountains in the winter season are often topped with ice and snow.

Can you add some skiers to this mountain and other wintery objects you might see?

Summer Season

What do you think the mountains look like in the summer?
What differences do you think you might see from winter?

Can you complete the picture below showing what you think
they would look like during the summer?

What sports might you see on the mountain in the summer?

Don't Get Lost!

Do you know which is North, East, South and West?
Using the compass, help this lost skier find his way to the
mountain hut where his friends are waiting for him:

Go North 2 places; Go East 6 places; Go North 1 place.
Circle the mountain hut you end up at.

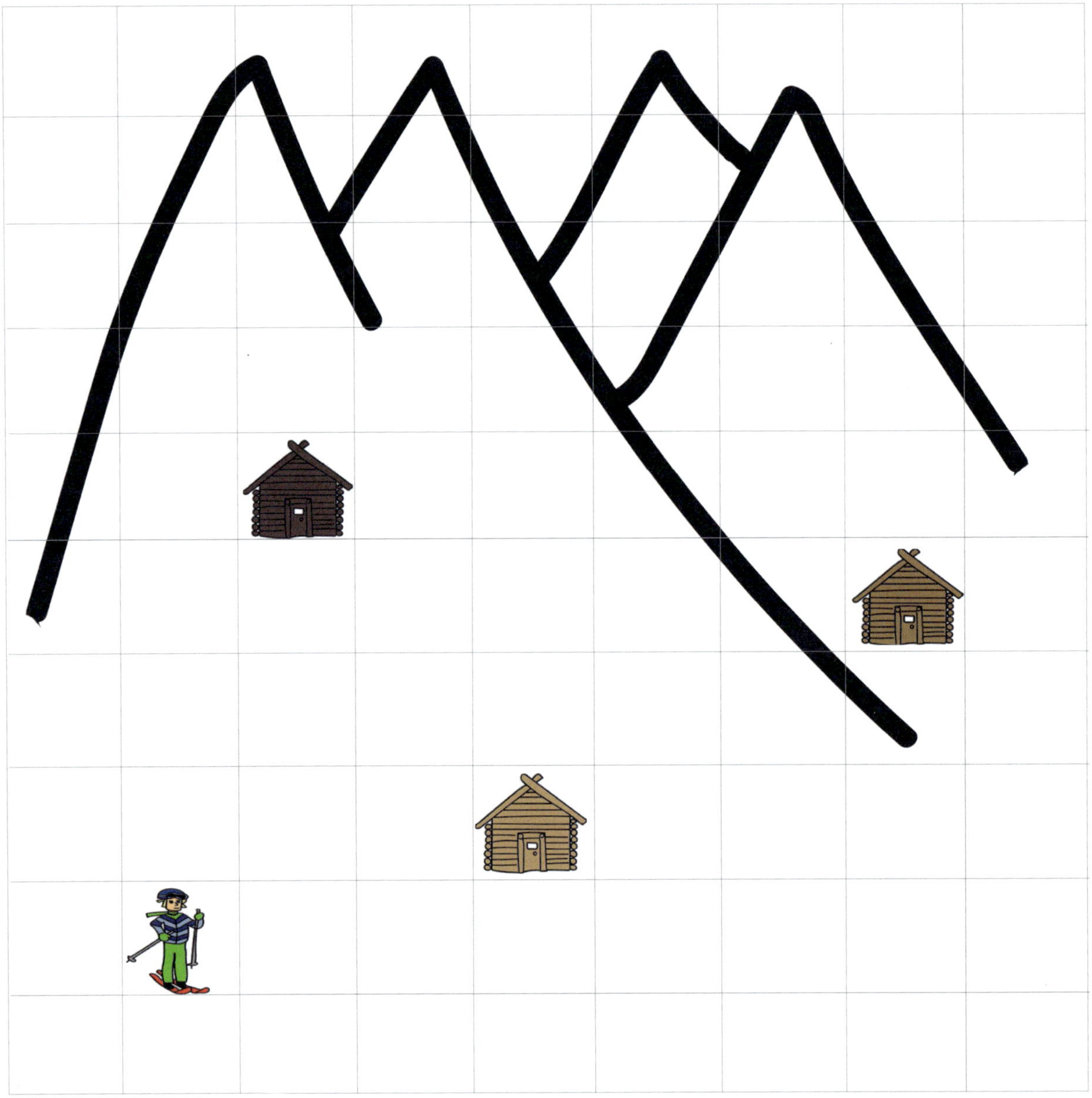

Find the Lost Skis

Can you note down the grid references of the lost skis?

 F3 ___   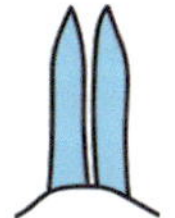 ___   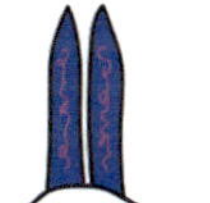 ___   ___

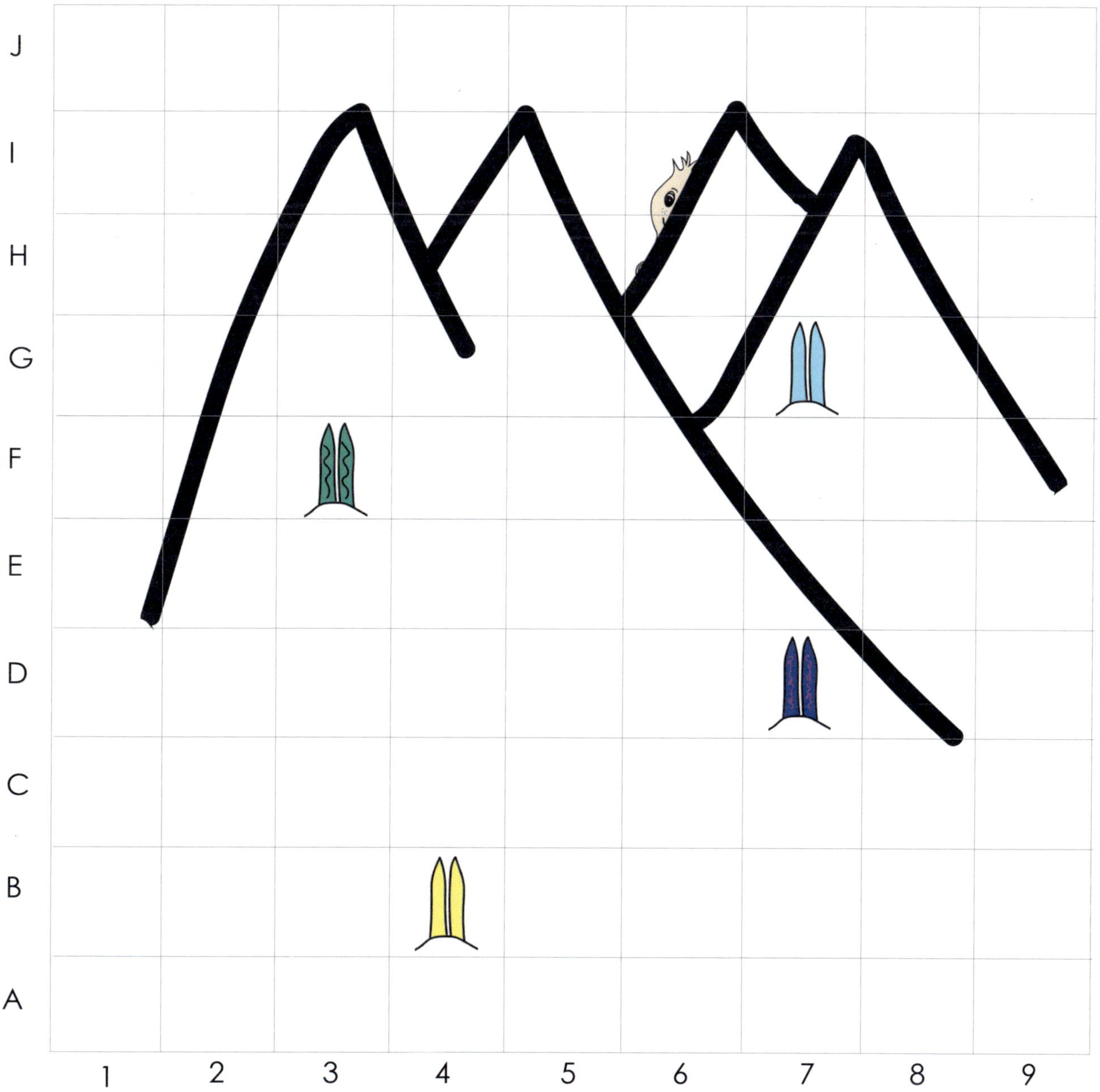

Last Lift

It's 4 o'clock. The ski lifts have started to close!

Find your way through the maze to the lift that's still open.
Good Luck!

Keeping Warm

What do you wear to keep warm when it's cold outside?

Can you complete this "warm clothes" puzzle?
Fill in the gaps in the grid. Each item must only appear ONCE in every row and column, so look carefully...

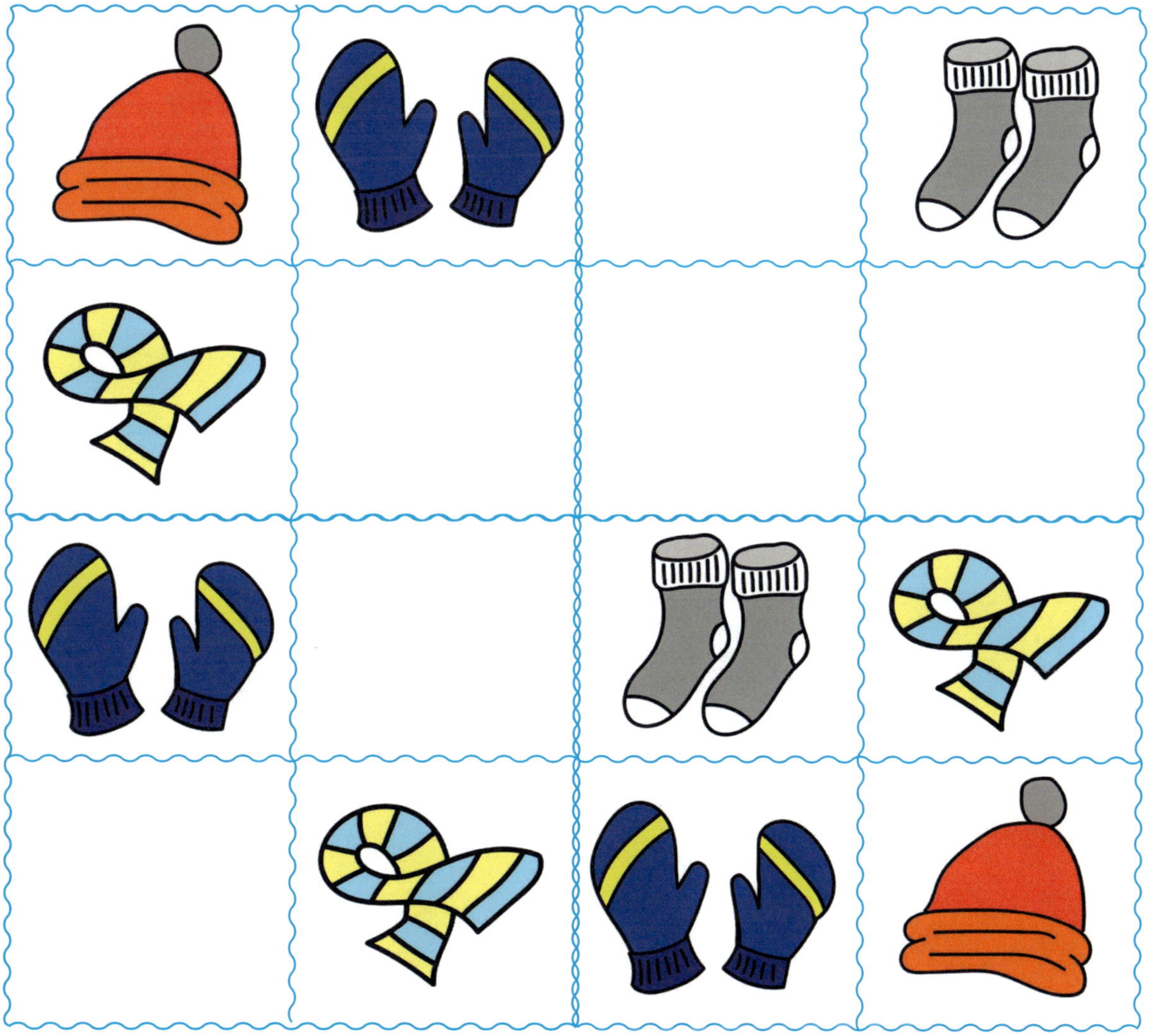

Alpine Trees

Can you use the grid to copy this picture into the grid on the opposite page accurately?

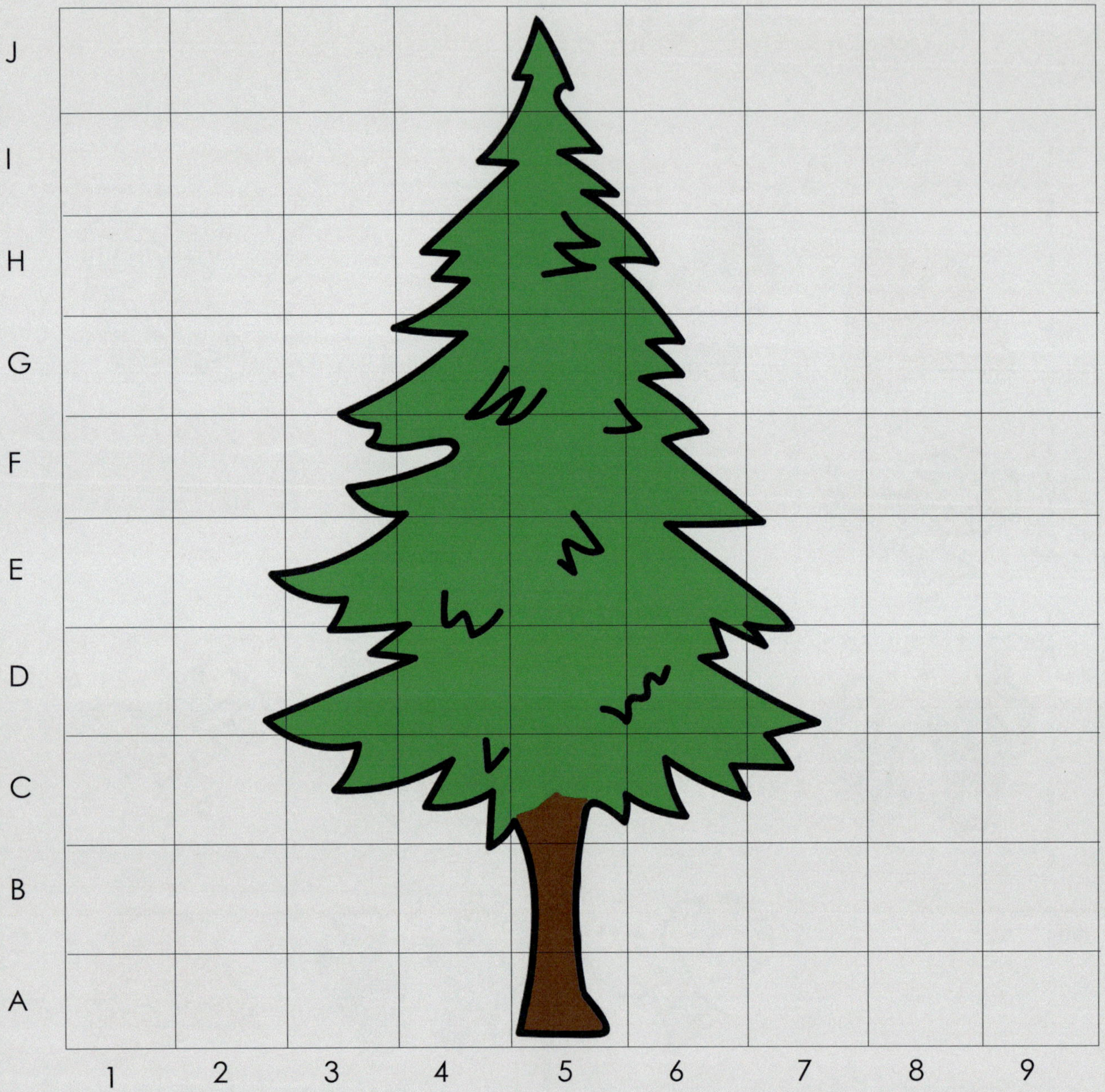

	1	2	3	4	5	6	7	8	9
J									
I									
H									
G									
F									
E									
D									
C									
B									
A									

Freezing Temperatures

When it's cold outside, water turns into ice!

Can you match these temperatures with the type of water you might find?

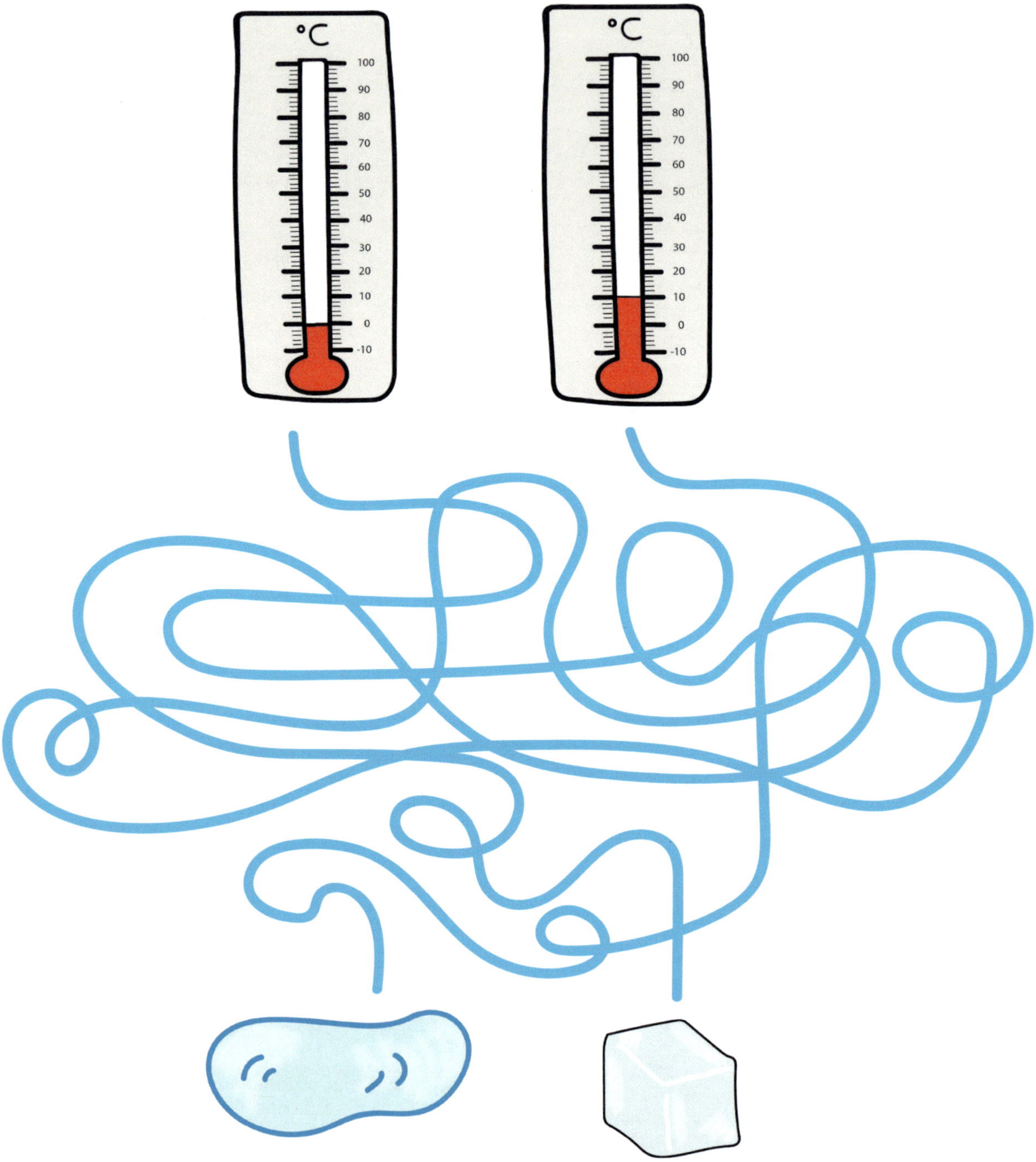

Icicles!

Have you spotted any icicles during your trip?
Icicles are made when water starts to melt and as the water drips off its surface, the cold air freezes it again into a giant frozen drip!

Can you measure and write how long these six icicles are in cm?

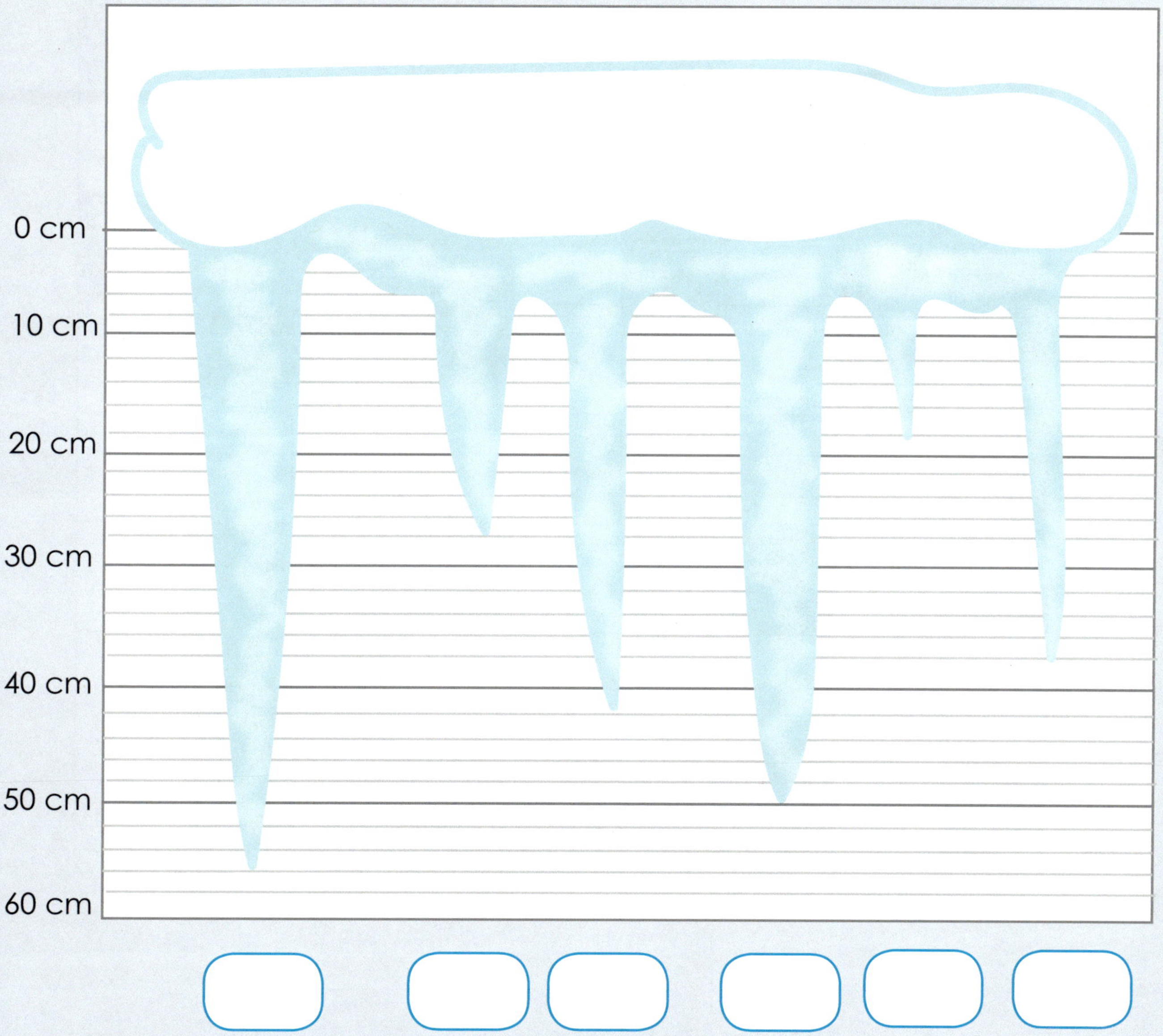

Fuelling Station

Warming up with some delicious food is an important part of a skiers day!

See if you can complete this foodie crossword using the picture clues below.

ACROSS

1 
2 
3 

DOWN

1 
2 
3 
4 

36

Memory Bank

It's time to write down all the things you've done, seen and tasted on your trip!

WRITE, DRAW, STAPLE, STICK

A Place to Stay

Where are you staying on your ski trip? Is it a hotel?
A house? A chalet? An apartment? Something else?

Can you **draw a picture** of it here?

Home Sweet Home

Can you draw a picture of where you live back at home?

What is different about this and your holiday home?

What have you eaten?

Draw some food you have eaten on holiday on the plate below.
What was your favourite?

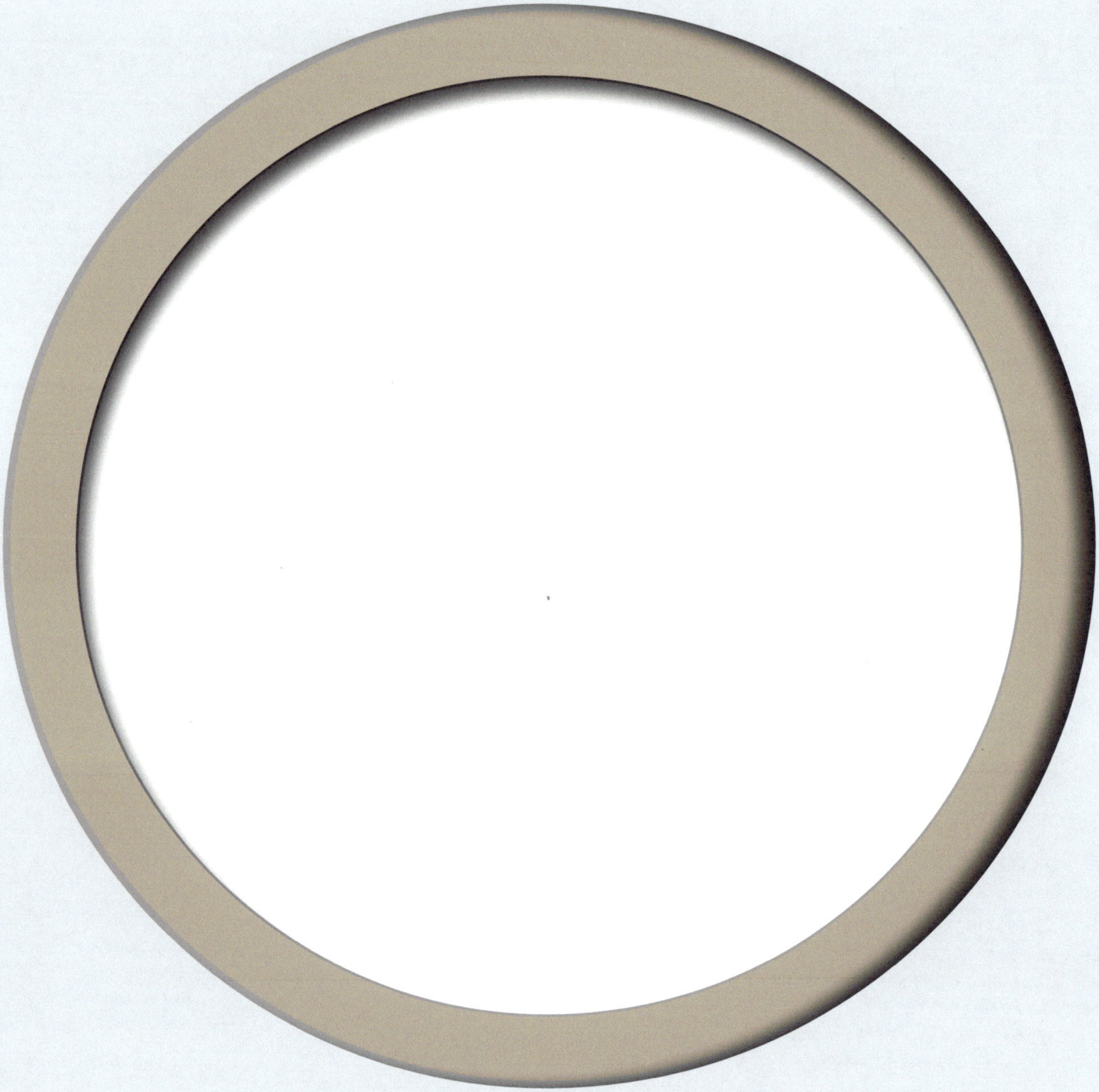

Write a postcard about your adventures, and design a nice stamp:

Cartolina Postale

Momento Collage

Stick bits and pieces on these pages that you've collected during your trip; favourite tickets, receipts, leaflets, drawings...

Daily Diary

Monday

Tuesday

Wednesday

Thursday

Friday

Saturday

Sunday

Memory Gallery

Draw pictures or doodles of any special memories:

The Good and The Bad

Time to think about the best bits and the worst bits:

What have been the **best three** things about your trip?

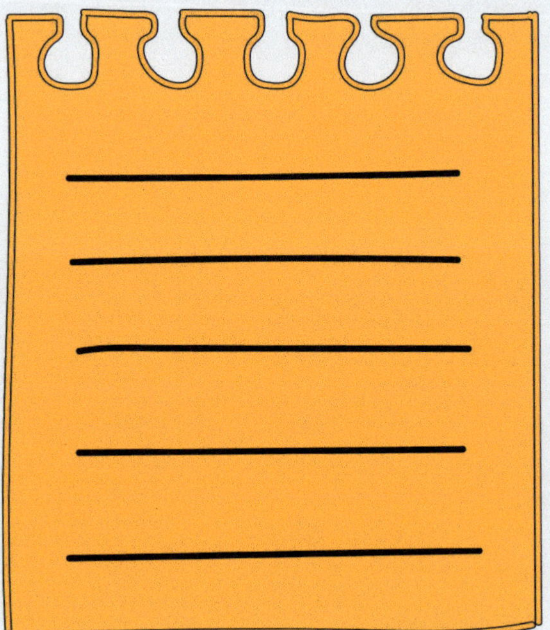

What have been the **worst three** things about your trip?

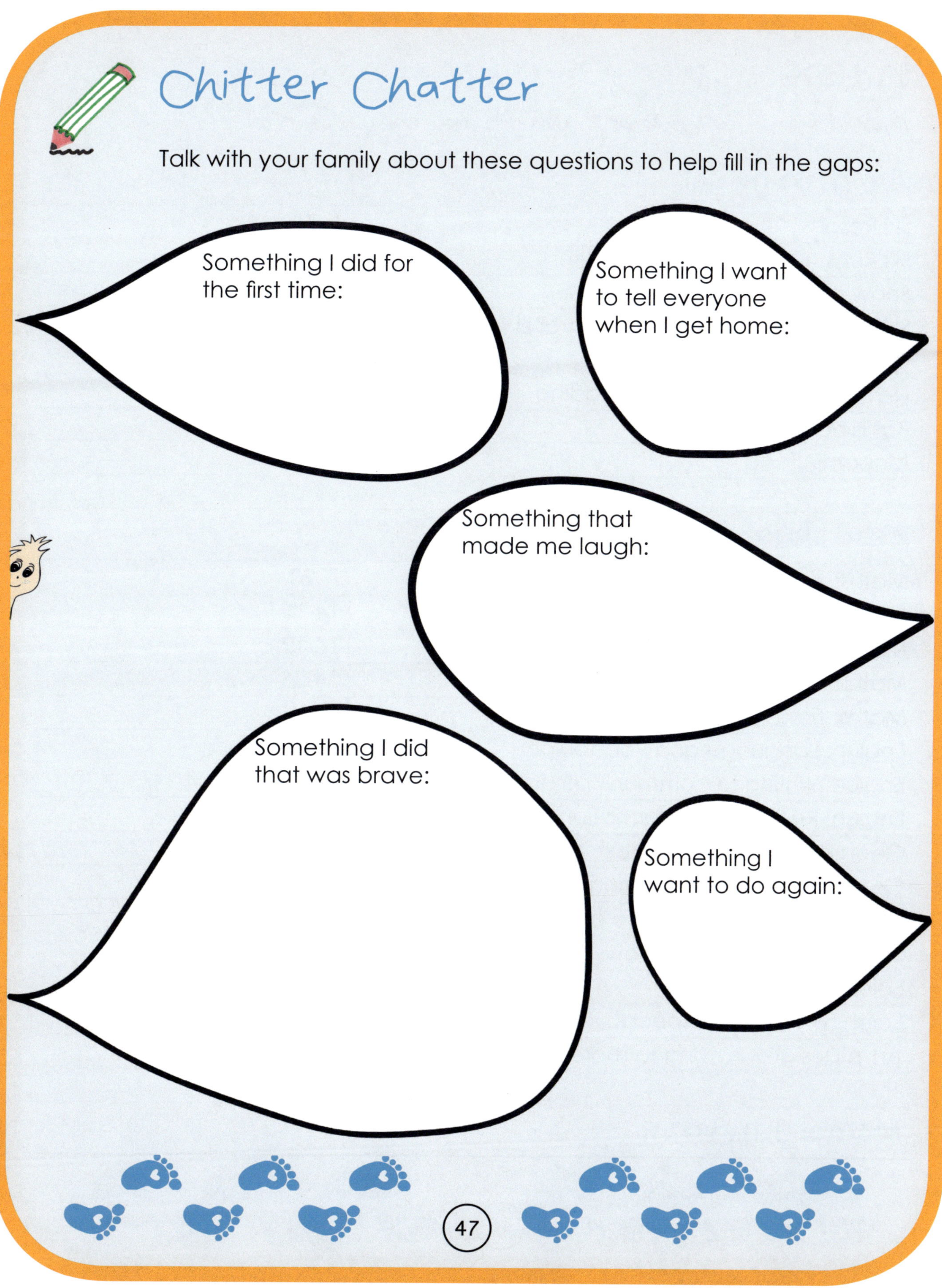

Chitter Chatter
Talk with your family about these questions to help fill in the gaps:
Something I did for the first time:
Something I want to tell everyone when I get home:
Something that made me laugh:
Something I did that was brave:
Something I want to do again:
47

Index

(what's in this book and where you can find it)

All things ski

Key skills

Memory making

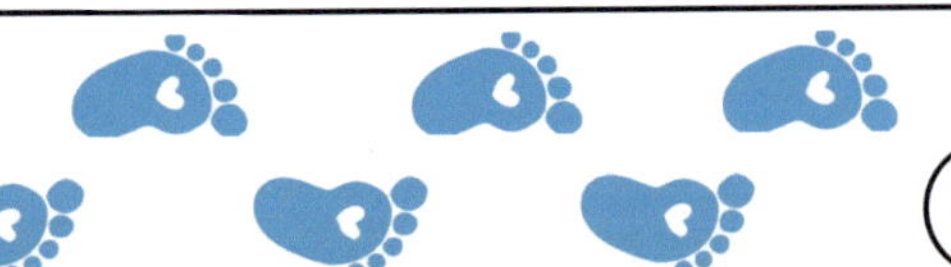

Au Revoir, Ciao, See ya later!

Spain

USA

Greece

France

Egypt

China

UK

Australia

South Africa

Thailand

Mexico

Finland

Made in the USA
Monee, IL
07 July 2026